funfacts about Hermit Crab

34 Frequently Asked Questions by

Crab Pet Owners & Lovers

Short Picture Book for Kids

BY FIONA WEBER

Introduction

What about keeping an animal that looks extremely singular, has curious behavior, and will be attentive to everything that happens? Hermit Crabs can be the perfect choice for you!

In addition to being an excellent species for beginners in animal keeping, it is a very easy species to maintain. All you need is a simple enclosure. Then, you can easily find them for sale in many species, colors, and patterns. Even with all the ease of having one of these crabs, you may still need to find out whether they are a good choice to keep as a pet. We made this exclusive ebook to solve your doubts, answering all common questions about the unique Hermit Crab.

1. Are Hermit Crabs, crabs?

In the zoological sense of the word, no.

The hermit crab or paguros, are crustaceans of the pagouridea or paguroidea family. There are more than 800 species of hermit crabs worldwide, also known as hermit crabs or paguros.

They need a shell to cover their abdomen, which is much softer than other crabs. Because of this soft abdomen, these animals are not considered true crabs.

2. Why are they called hermit crabs?

Their unique relationship with their shells made these crabs famous and gave them the name hermit. As the animal's body grows, it needs to change shells, as it needs more space.

They are crabs that lack protection for their abdomen, so they seek protection using shells

abandoned by other dead mollusks; this behavior is called thanatocresis. The hermit crab's abdomen curls up to fit the chosen shell and uses its legs and claws to block the entrance to its home. Although it has an unprotected stomach, the rest of its body is protected by a rigid exoskeleton, so the body part outside the shell is protected from predators.

3. Where do Hermit Crabs live?

As an incredibly large group, these crabs occur virtually all over the tropical part of the world, in freshwater, saltwater, and even terrestrial environments.

4. What is the Hermit Crab's lifespan?

As we find different species being kept as pets, the lifespan depends on the species we are

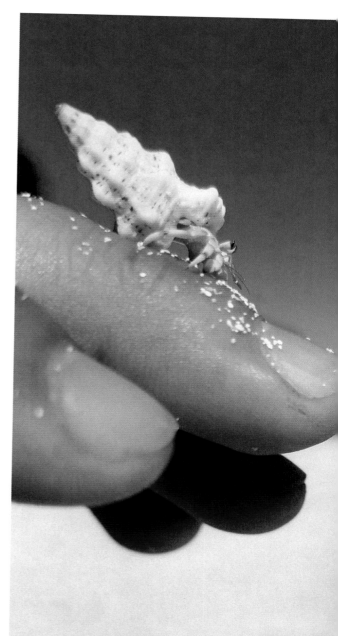

referring to.

Some species, such as those found in saltwater aquariums, can live for a short time, less than one year. Other species, like land crabs, can live for more than 25 years.

Your crab can live many years if it has enough space, enough life quality, and a balanced diet.

5. What types of Hermit Crabs can I find for sale?

You can find more than a dozen species available in stores and from specialized sellers. Some are rare and more complex to keep, but we have some species that are more prevalent and easier to keep as pets. Among the most common species, we can mention some land crabs belonging to the genus Coenobita, with the species Strawberry Hermit Crab, Ecuadorian Hermit Crab, Caribbean Hermit Crab, Australian

Land Hermit Crab, and Blueberry Hermit Crab being the most common to see. Other species of the same genus are also widely available.

In saltwater aquariums, especially those representing coral reefs, these crabs are widely used as ornamentation and cleaning crew, keeping the aquarium free of wastes and unwanted algae.

Among the main species, we can find crabs of the genus Clibanarius, such as the Dwarf Red Tip Hermit Crab and Dwarf Blue Leg Hermit Crab, and Paguristes, such as the Scarlet Reef Hermit Crab.

6. Where do the Hermit Crabs get its shell?

The final portion of the hermit crab's body, the abdomen, is not protected by a natural shell, the exoskeleton, as in other crabs. Because of this, they need to go after armor, so they don't become lunch for a marine predator like octopuses.

The solution found by hermit crabs could not be better: they carefully search for empty mollusk shells on the ocean floor. Then, they try on shells as people try new shoes until they find the perfect size to protect them.

As they grow, these crabs abandon the old shell and search for a new, larger one. In addition, hermit crabs sometimes make armor upgrades with extra protection from sea anemones.

Their shells are essential to the crab's life, which cannot survive if it is naked. In addition to protecting against predators, the cover helps the animal maintain its humidity and temperature, protecting against environmental factors such as light and heat.

7. How often does a hermit crab change shells?

Changing shells depends on the crab species and the animal's environment, age, and health. For example, as the change of shell occurs due to growth, young animals change shells faster than older animals. In these cases, the animal can change shells 1 to 2 times a year.

Older animals may change shells once every 12 or even 18 months. Another issue is the availability of the shell. The crab will not switch shells until it knows new homes are waiting for it.

8. Are Hermit Crabs good pets?

As strange as they may seem, they are curious animals and easy to care for, which makes them almost perfect pets. These crabs are highly docile and don't need significant structures or a lot of work to stay healthy and happy.

It is an excellent acquisition for tanks with other animals and even a good companion for humans, including children. Just offer them a space and healthy food to make them happy.

9. Are Hermit Crabs easy to care for?

Hermit Crabs are trendy as they are adorable,

active, and curious pets. In addition, they live well in small apartments, are not very expensive, and care is not costly. For families with children, these crabs are excellent pets. However, before deciding to own one of these crabs, you must ensure that you can provide the new family member with a suitable life for a long time.

Terrestrial species need adequate space with access to water. You can keep aquatic species as well as fish in tropical aquariums.

They are effortless to keep animals, perfect for beginners and experienced hobbyists alike.

10. How do Hermit Crabs behave?

These crabs are highly curious and a little fearful. They may take some time to feel comfortable in new environments, but they always keep an eye on

everything around them. They can spend long periods buried, especially when they are about to molt.

Some species can be very territorial and can fight among themselves. Others like to steal shells from their companions.

Land hermit crabs appropriately abandon snail shells and make them their homes. However, empty shells are often filled with soil. As a result, they cannot enter them, so they remove other crabs from their shells, as they can remodel their shells, sometimes doubling the internal volume.

This provides:

More room to grow.

More space for the eggs.

Protection from dragging while on the move.

Since empty snail shells are rare on land, the best hope for moving into a new home is to drive others out of their shells. When three or more land crabs come together, they quickly attract dozens of others eager to vie for the new shell. They usually form a line of battle, from smallest to largest, each holding the crab in front of him, and once one hapless crab is ripped from its shell, at the same time, the others move on to larger shells.

Overall, they are very docile, curious, and interactive animals.

11. Will my Hermit Crab

love me?
Not exactly.
These animals have a great sense of the world, and they may even recognize you and create some kind of bond, as they will associate you with food or something.
New studies suggest that these animals may have some types of feelings, but creating love for their owner is already unlikely.

12. Are Hermit Crabs boring?

It's up to you.
Some people find these animals boring, while others see these crabs as spectacular animals full of personality.
They are animals with distinct beauty and always draw attention to their behavior. Species kept mainly as pets or ornamentals have beautiful, striking colors, making them highly eye-catching.
Altogether, they are exceptional animals, combining a beautiful beauty with a behavior very different from other animals.

13. Can my Hermit Crab pinch me?

Yes, they definitely will pinch you.
The pinch can be caused by several factors and is rarely a form of aggression.
They will pinch you when they feel insecure, especially during handling,

when they feel unsteady on the ground or because they are trying to defend themselves, thinking your hand is an aggressor. And yes, depending on the size of the crab, it could hurt you. If this occurs, immediately place the animal on a solid and level surface; if this is not enough, move the animal slightly on this surface. This will give the crab confidence to feel secure and let you go.

14. Are Hermit Crabs poisonous?

If your pet pinches you, rest assured that they are not poisonous and do not have enough power to cause extensive damage. These animals hardly

transmit diseases; if one of them hurts you, wash it with soap in running water, and everything will be fine.

15. How long can Hermit Crabs live without water?

These animals are directly dependent on the relative humidity of the environment; if they do not have access to water, most terrestrial species will perish within 24 to 72 hours.

Most aquatic crab species should never be exposed to dry places; if this happens, they will perish in a short time.

16. What are the pros and cons of keeping a Hermit Crab?

The main reason for keeping these animals and their unique beauty and behavior is having a beautiful aquarium decorated with one or more of these animals in your living room or bedroom. It is undoubtedly something unique and very cool, in addition to being an animal with a long lifespan, staying with you for years.

Another positive point is that they are effortless and cheap to keep animals, requiring a few minutes daily dedicated to their well-being.

Another cool thing is that, with the advancement of technology, you can print shells with different colors and characteristics according to the size of your pet.

The main downside is that these crabs do not form bonds with their owner or do not interact as much as birds or mammals. Having shells always available can also be a problem, as you must always be attentive and provide your pet with several shells of different sizes. Finally, a factor limiting the maintenance of these animals is to offer terrariums that have a part of water; in some cases, it can be a complicated construction. And, if this water is stagnant, it needs a lot of maintenance so it doesn't develop strong odors.

17. What do I need to keep my Hermit Crab healthy?

The main thing is that you know as much as possible about the species you want to keep.

Caring for hermit crabs can be easier than caring for a fish tank. The materials needed to care for hermit crabs are simple. A place to shelter, food, water, and a clean, warm, humid environment are all your hermit crab needs.

With the proper care and supplies for these little animals, hermit crabs will live very well and for a long time.

You will need an aquarium, or a terrarium, where hermit crabs can live. Glass or acrylic aquariums or terrariums work best because, in addition to having good transparency, they are easy to keep clean. It is also important that the aquarium has a lid; this way, it avoids leaks and helps maintain the humidity in the environment.

Hermit crab habitat (also known as crabitat – "crab habitat") will follow a pattern of humidity concentration, which should remain between 70 and 80 percent, with a temperature between 71 and 78 degrees F. You can regulate humidity and temperature through a heater placed beneath

the hermit crab's habitat and a fogger or air pump connected to an air outlet inside the water.

The aquarium will need to have a substrate placed at the bottom. Sand is an excellent option because it's easy for crabs to dig. Extra shells are always needed because crabs grow and need to exchange their shells. Shells should have oval or circular openings, at least the size of crab claws. There should always be two shells of each size for the hermit crab to choose from. Never force a crab out of its shell.

Before being placed in the crab's habitat, You must boil the shells in ordinary dechlorinated tap water with a bit of salt.

It is essential to boil these shells as they may contain bacteria, which could kill the crabs; applying heat will kill any bacteria or

germs.

You should give food and water to hermit crabs. As with other animals, you can use dishes and bowls for this purpose without any problems. The main thing to remember is that the water containers must be large enough for the largest hermit crab to enter.

The freshwater available to these animals must be dechlorinated. You can use tap water if treated with a water conditioner found in stores or aquarium supply stores. You can also use bottled water if it comes from a natural source.

Some hermit crabs also need salt water but don't use table salt. Instead, use aquarium sea salt, which is safe for hermit crabs and can be found in aquarium supply stores or sections. Salt water must also be dechlorinated

before use in crabitat. Place sponges, decorations, rocks, or logs in freshwater or saltwater containers so the smaller hermit crabs can escape them without drowning. Other supplies needed in the crabitat are structures the hermit crab can use for shelter. Hermit crabs are nocturnal animals, so they will need a space to escape the daily activities around them.

Many types of shelter are available for hermit crabs, from coconut shells to hollow logs. In addition, you'll often find precisely what your hermit crab needs in the aquarium section of pet supply stores.

Also, look for other crabitat accessories, such as places for the hermit crab to climb. Large pieces of cork, driftwood, or coral are great for crabitat because the crab not only clings to them but also "snacks" these materials. Light woods, wicker baskets, and crab nets will also do well in your hermit crab's habitat. Hermit crab care includes more than just crabitat breeding. You will need to check the temperature and humidity daily and remove any leftover food from the night before. You will also want to know if the crabs are digging and burying themselves in the sand. If they don't return and feed daily, they are very likely to be molting.

Weekly, the hermit crab owner will have to replace the fresh and saltwater, change or clean the sponges (if using them) and clean the food and water bowls.

Lastly, every six months, the crabitat should be thoroughly cleaned, the sand cleaned or replaced, the decorations washed, and any wood used placed in the microwave for about two minutes.

18. Do I need fresh or salty water to keep my Hermit Crab?
Except for strictly freshwater species, it is correct to offer fresh and saltwater for your crab. These animals need fresh water to drink and salt water baths to stay healthy.

19. Is it better to keep more than one Hermit crab?

Yes, for sure!

If you decide to keep hermit crabs, you should know that most species like to live in a community. That's why it's always advisable to keep a group.

Remember that the number of animals must be consistent with the available space; the more individuals, the more needed space.

20. Can my Hermit Crab kill its tankmates?

Yes, for sure.

Some species cannot live with others because of aggressiveness or territorialism. For example, terrestrial species may kill others for territory or steal their shells.

It is also common to attack crabs that are molting or changing shells, including cannibalism.

21. Can my Hermit Crab live with fish?

Yes, without problems.

The vast majority of species can be kept with fish without any problems, as they are not predators. However, in some rare cases, crabs can eat fish; this is usually a sign of a deficiency in the crab's diet.

On the contrary, avoid placing your crabs with fish or other large predatory animals, as they will probably be a great snack.

22. What is the best food for my Hermit Crab?

Hermit crabs are omnivorous animals that eat pretty much everything.

The variety of foods consumed in their diet often varies depending on the availability of food in their habitat and the time of year.

Therefore, it will be vital to provide your hermit crab with complete and balanced nutrition based on its nutritional needs.

In the wild, they eat other smaller crustaceans such as snails, mussels, or shrimp, worms, the remains of any dead animals they find, and plant remains.

In an aquarium, they will adapt to eating pieces of fish, mussels, or shrimp, but we can also provide them with vegetables and pieces of fruit.

You should know what foods your hermit crabs can and should consume.

Feeding hermit crabs have become a universal discussion regarding what to use to feed them.

According to some hermit crab owners, you should not use commercial pet food because it contains ingredients that eventually kill the hermit crabs.

These owners use only natural foods, such as raw or cooked meats, without using any seasonings.

However, suppose you decide to feed it natural foods. In that case, it is crucial to maintain a balanced meal, offering meat, fruits, and vegetables.

Always consider keeping in touch with a veterinarian you trust, formulating the best possible diet for your hermit crab, and ensuring it has a long, happy and healthy life!

23. Which fruits and vegetables can I offer to my Hermit Crab?

In the wild, hermit crabs have an incredibly diverse diet.

These crabs love all types of plant matter. They can eat practically everything. You can offer coconuts, mangoes, apples, and many other fruits. However, avoid only citrus fruits such as lemons and oranges.

Leaves like endive, spinach, kale, and cabbage can also be offered. Remember to offer only fresh leaves.

Vegetables like broccoli, carrots, bell peppers, eggplant, and carrots are delicious and great treats. In addition to providing several nutrients, they also help color the crabs.

You should strongly avoid offering garlic and onions. Remember to offer the food of organic origin and adequately sanitized, free of chemicals and other products.

24. Which food should I avoid offering to my Hermit Crab?

As much as these crabs eat everything, we should never offer anything that will directly attack the animal's life.

Avoid condiments and salty and spicy foods.

Never offer onions, garlic, and citrus fruits; these can harm your crab.

Never offer processed or human foods such as fat, salt, or sugar-rich foods like snacks, chocolates, tortillas, etc.

25. How often should I feed my Hermit Crab?

Many questions are asked about feeding crabs in captivity.

You can feed your hermit crabs daily without any problems.

Daily feeding decreases predation from tank mates and some types of aggression.

You can feed adult crabs every two days. Still, they are animals constantly feeding on different materials they find in their environment.

The idea is always to provide a balanced diet, but you must observe some critical factors.

26. What is molting in Hermit Crab?

A critical evolutionary achievement of arthropods, the exoskeleton (from the Greek éx , "outer; external") is a rigid structure that entirely or partially covers the body of these animals, protecting Organs internal organs and support to the musculature.

As the animal grows throughout its life cycle, this exoskeleton is shed, a process called ecdysis or molting.

Ecdysis can occur several times in an animal's life, an unlimited number that varies from species to species. The action of two hormones dictates the mechanism: ecdysone, which plays the role of stimulating the epithelial cells to start the process of ecdysis; and the Moulting Inhibitor Hormone (MIH), which, as its name already explains, acts contrary to ecdysone. The entire cycle takes place in 4 steps:

1st. Pro-ecdysis - a stage that precedes the molt, in which the animal prepares to release an exoskeleton, replacing it with another. At this stage, the animal's body retains water and air, which facilitates its support during the exchange and exerts pressure that helps to break the old carapace.

2nd. Ecdysis - effective exchange of exoskeletons, the stage in which the old skeleton is discarded, giving way to a new one.

3rd. Post-ecdysis - stage after the molt, in which the animal increases in size and has its new exoskeleton gradually hardened.

4th. Intermolt - comprises the period between one

molt and another, in which the animal stores nutrients to prepare for the restart of the entire cycle. The effective growth of the animal occurs at this stage.

Two environmental factors significantly interfere with this cycle: temperature and nutrient availability. In addition, the temperature variation alters the animal's metabolism, which can anticipate or postpone the process. As the animal needs a lot of energy to carry out the molt, there must also be good availability of nutrients. However, suppose the amount of food available is insufficient. In that case, the molt is delayed because, in this way, the animal cannot supply the energy expenditure after the process.

With the aging of the animal and the reach of its reproductive activity, its ability to carry out shell changes ceases. This happens because, before adulthood, the animal uses energy from food for its growth. In contrast, at sexual age, this energy will be necessary for producing organs and reproductive cells.

In addition to being a significant aspect of the evolution of arthropods, ecdysis also represents an essential adaptive value since it allows the adaptation of these animals to several different types of environments. On the other hand, this property can damage the living being since, after the molt, the animal is vulnerable for a certain period (due to high energy expenditure), which facilitates the attack of natural predators.

The hermit crab starts looking for its first shell to protect its body when it has already developed its four antennae and two claws. He sheds his skin frequently during this growth process until he reaches the megalopa stage. To change the shells, the hermit crab must break its old shell, and it needs to enlarge its body. It absorbs water until it gains 70% of its weight. Once her old shell is broken, she looks for one big enough to fit in and leave room to grow.

27. What to do when my Hermit Crab is molting?

The molting period for these animals is highly stressful and is accompanied by significant behavioral changes.

The main change we see in these crabs is that they try to stay hidden, mostly buried, and they also stop feeding. At the first signs of molting, some keepers place their crabs in isolation tanks, where they can carry out their exchange with the certainty that nothing wrong will happen to them.

When the animal is in this period, any sudden change in environmental parameters or any stress can cause irreversible damage, and even the death of your crab, so the best way to deal with this molting period is to let your crab quiet without interference and without touching your pet.

28. Which are some of the most common Hermit Crab diseases?

Hermit crabs are incredibly hardy animals, but some diseases can affect them.

Unfortunately, there are few studies on this topic and few known conditions. Below we will cite the illnesses most commonly found in these animals. Remember never to self-medicate your crabs, as these animals are susceptible to different drugs and substances.

- Shell disease is probably the most common condition in these animals and is found in several species of crustaceans. It is caused by an infection (usually bacterial, but it can be viral) that degrades the shell of these animals. This degradation causes discolorations and lesions on the animal's carapace and can even lead to death. The infection is left behind by carrying out the process of molting and exchanging the shell.

- Mites: Mites are small parasitic arthropods that live on the surface of crabs. These animals stress your pet and can generate secondary conditions such as anemia. These parasites are easily seen with the naked eye, which facilitates diagnosis. As a treatment, you should give your crab a bath of total submersion, as well as proceed with the complete cleaning of the room in which he lives, changing the substrate, cleaning all the glasses deeply, and boiling all the decorations. If any mite or egg exists in the environment, reinfestation will occur. Therefore, it is important to quarantine new animals, so we reduce contamination and treatment to a small quarantine tank.

- Fungal infections are an

unfortunately widespread and highly contagious type of infection; if you see this in one of your animals, it should be immediately isolated. It is easily distinguishable, as it forms white spots on the crab's surface. As a treatment, you should proceed with a bath submerged in salt water, cleaning everything in the crab's environment and changing the substrate.

29. Why is my Hermit Crab weak?

If your crab appears weak or very tired, this is a sign that something is not right and deserves your attention.

Some factors can cause this behavior; among the main ones is some grip on the gill of these animals, something like suffocation. In addition, this can be caused by some toxic product in the aquarium (such as chlorine in the water, for example) or even low humidity.

It can also signify stress caused by competition for territory or food.

And, last and least worryingly, it could just be a sign that molting is approaching.

Either way, it's a behavior that needs your careful attention and observation.

30. How can I know that my Hermit Crab is healthy?

Please get to know your animal and be constantly watching and attentive to its behaviors, especially at feeding times. Only then will you know if your pet is healthy.

Healthy crabs will be active and curious, showing their coloring in perfect condition, feeding, and demonstrating their usual behaviors.

Any change in this pattern requires your attention to be redoubled.

31. Why is my Hermit crab burying itself?

It's normal behavior.

They bury themselves for some reasons, mainly due to the environment's excessive temperature and to protect themselves from predators, especially during the molting period. Others are bored, digging through the substrate and looking for some tidbit to pass the time.

32. Why is my Hermit Crab out of its shell and not moving?

This behavior could mean

two things.
Either your crab is doing its molting, or it's dead.

33. Why is my Hermit Crab not eating?

This is a clear sign of molting.
Rest assured, your crab will shed its skin, prepare a calm environment, and keep it in peace.

34. Is my Hermit crab dying?

The signs these crabs show when dying are very similar to the symptoms of molting, basically being immobile out of the shell. The first thing to do is to carefully observe the hermit crab & see if it shows any movement and how long it has been in this state. These animals usually show short and fast signs when molting, which are difficult to perceive.
If it's not moving, and it's been like that for a long time, the crab is most likely dead. A tip is to be guided by the smell, as these animals quickly enter a state of decomposition, exhaling a strong and undesirable odor.

Common Care Mistakes

at home is not just a responsibility for the specimen but the entire ecosystem. As dozens of surveys indicate, thousands of species

1. Getting a pet impulsively.

The world of crabs is as fascinating as hermit crabs themselves. Many exotic animals are kept as pets, but not all adapt well to life in captivity; some need a lot of space and special feeding. To this is added the fact that some of these animals are taken from their natural environment to be sold, which is unethical and harmful to the environment.

Having a hermit crab

of exotic animals are at risk of disappearing, partly due to the sale and removal of adult individuals from their natural environment.

If you want to have one of these crabs at home, you should always check the origin of the animal. Never buy or adopt an animal on impulse without first thinking about and preparing everything the animal needs. For example, think that when you acquire a crab, it will be under your care for more than a decade, and you must have the social and financial conditions to keep them healthy all that time.

Acquiring any animal as a pet without evaluating the fundamental conditions to keep it leads to neglect and abandonment.

2. Problems with choosing your first Hermit Crab

First, if you still need to gain experience with these animals, research extensively on the crab species that best suits your habits and possibilities.

Always get animals from well-known breeders with a good reputation, ask to meet the parents, and observe to see if all animals are healthy if the sick are separated and how the breeder takes care of his animals.

3. Common mistakes with housing and keeping Hermit Crabs

Always maintain the ideal humidity and temperature for your crabs. This is the main mistake experienced tutors and novices alike make. Another mistake we see a lot is the need for proper ventilation. Remember that they are animals from tropical places that need water and also enjoy some vertical spaces, so avoid elements of desertic terrariums like cactus plants. Instead, always offer rocks, and have both fresh and saltwater available for it.

Make sure to keep the terrarium always sanitized and with good ventilation; this prevents the spreading diseases such as fungi and mites.

When maintaining a group, or an environment with crabs and other animals, keep an eye out for food, territory, and aggression. Once again, we emphasize the importance of being attentive during feeding. When feeding them, provide the amount of food the crabs will consume at that moment, and never leave food for later. Remember only to offer vegetables that have been adequately cleaned or have residues of any substance. As well as meats without processing or with some seasoning.

4. Controlling diseases, illnesses, and other conditions

The vast majority of diseases and illnesses in captive crabs are caused by poor management of the animal and its environment. Because of this, we consistently reinforce the importance of knowing and keeping an eye on your animals and having specialists' help. In this regard, we have some recommendations:

- Habitat conditions: Crabs depend on a controlled environment to keep a healthy metabolism. Therefore, any change can have severe consequences for their health. However, the parameters of temperature and humidity are the ones that most impact the animal.

- Diet: Maintaining the proper diet to achieve a healthy and perfect crab. This factor is crucial because an adequate diet keeps the body vigorous and allows it to face pathologies. In addition, a wide variety of nutritional problems can cost the crab its life.

- Hygiene: Keeping your pet's environment clean and free of feces and leftover food is essential when keeping animals in captivity. In this way, we mainly avoid the spread of disease and the low immunity of animals. Therefore, maintain an impeccable cleaning routine. Always sanitize your hands before and after cleaning their environment or holding them in your hand.

- Accidents: Any physical injury suffered by the animal can lead to severe pathology, so treating it promptly and correctly is better.

In this book, we covered the most common questions to successfully keeping a unique Hermit Crab and a great Hermit Crab enclosure. Hopefully, you now have a better idea of what it is like to keep a Hermit Crab as a pet.

As you can see, Hermit Crabs are animals with no secrets to keep. With easy-to-understand behavior, you will quickly become an expert in these types of crabs. If you like to keep super calm and friendly crabs, prepare your cage and go for these incredible Hermit Crabs!

Hermit Crab Word Search

Find and circle the words.

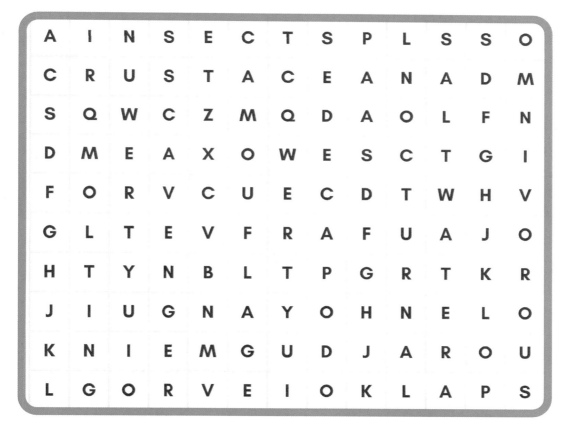

A	I	N	S	E	C	T	S	P	L	S	S	O
C	R	U	S	T	A	C	E	A	N	A	D	M
S	Q	W	C	Z	M	Q	D	A	O	L	F	N
D	M	E	A	X	O	W	E	S	C	T	G	I
F	O	R	V	C	U	E	C	D	T	W	H	V
G	L	T	E	V	F	R	A	F	U	A	J	O
H	T	Y	N	B	L	T	P	G	R	T	K	R
J	I	U	G	N	A	Y	O	H	N	E	L	O
K	N	I	E	M	G	U	D	J	A	R	O	U
L	G	O	R	V	E	I	O	K	L	A	P	S

CRUSTACEAN   SCAVENGER   OMNIVOROUS

CAMOUFLAGE   INSECTS   DECAPOD

NOCTURNAL   MOLTING   SALTWATER

Solution at Page 45

Download Five
Hermit Crab Posters

Scan w/your Camera to Download!

A Message From The Author

Hello from Oliver and her mom! We're the creators of The World of Rare Pets series of books.

Our hope is that you and your loved ones enjoy each and every book we create. It's our mission to reduce impulsive buying of rare pets & educate children beforehand so that they know what it's like to keep a pet responsibly.

We are no big publishing house with tons of money to throw in marketing efforts, so the only way to spread the word about our books is you, our lovely customers. If you like our book, please consider giving us your **honest feedback with a review on Amazon.** When you post a review on Amazon it really makes a huge difference towards helping a small business like ours.

We sincerely appreciate your purchase and for supporting our small business.

References

Angel, J. E. (2000). Effects of shell fit on the biology of the hermit crab Pagurus longicarpus (Say). Journal of Experimental Marine Biology and Ecology, 243(2), 169-184.

Bertness, M. D. (1981). Conflicting advantages in resource utilization: the hermit crab housing dilemma. The American Naturalist, 118(3), 432-437.

Buckley, W. J., & Ebersole, J. P. (1994). Symbiotic organisms increase the vulnerability of a hermit crab to predation. Journal of Experimental Marine Biology and Ecology, 182(1), 49-64.

Bundhitwongrut, T. (2018). Unregulated trade in land hermit crabs in Thailand. Natural History Bulletin of the Siam Society, 63, 27-40.

Childress, J. R. (1972). Behavioral ecology and fitness theory in a tropical hermit crab. Ecology, 53(5), 960-964.

Flesner, T. Food Preference in the Purple Pincher Hermit Crab (Coenobita clypeatus) Food Preference in the Purple Pincher Hermit Crab (Coenobita clypeatus).

Hazlett, B. A. (1981). The behavioral ecology of hermit crabs. Annual Review of Ecology and Systematics, 12, 1-22.

Helfman, G. S. (1977). Agonistic Behaviour of the Coconut Crab, Birgus latro (L.) 1. Zeitschrift für Tierpsychologie, 43(4), 425-438.

Hutagalung, R. A., Adrian, R., & Prasasty, D. (2020). The improvement of survival rate of land hermit crabs Coenobita (Malacostraca: Coenobitidae) in artificial habitat through multispecies and niche heterogeneity approach. In IOP Conference Series: Earth and Environmental Science (Vol. 404, No. 1, p. 012087). IOP Publishing.

Hutagalung, R. A., Koswara, N. W., & Prasasty, V. D. (2019, May). Improving the survival rate of land hermit crabs (Coenobita rugosus) through artificial habitat design. In IOP Conference Series: Earth and Environmental Science (Vol. 278, No. 1, p. 012036). IOP Publishing.

Hutagalung, R. A., Magdalena, S., Iskandar, I., & Mastrorillo, S. (2017). Increasing growth and survival rate of land hermit crabs (Coenobita sp.) in artificial habitat through feeding habit. International Journal of Applied and Physical Sciences, 3(3), 55-59.

Markham, J. C. (1968). Notes on growth-patterns and shell-utilization of the hermit crab Pagurus bernhardus (L.). Ophelia, 5(2), 189-205.

McLaughlin, P. A. (1983). Hermit Crabs are They Really Polyphyletic?. Journal of Crustacean Biology, 3(4), 608-621.

McMAHON, B. R., & BURGGREN, W. W. (1979). Respiration and adaptation to the terrestrial habitat in the land hermit crab Coenobita clypeatus. Journal of Experimental Biology, 79(1), 265-281.

Sanda, T., Hamasaki, K., Dan, S., & Kitada, S. (2019). Expansion of the northern geographical distribution of land hermit crab populations: colonization and overwintering success of Coenobita purpureus on the coast of the Boso Peninsula, Japan. Zoological studies, 58.

Spaulding, E. G. (1904). An establishment of association in hermit crabs, Eupagurus longicarpus. Journal of Comparative Neurology and Psychology, 14(1), 49-61.

Ster, I. (1988). Pagurus bernhardus (L.)—an

introduction to the natural history of hermit crabs. Field Studies, 7, 189-238.

THACKER, R. W. (1998). Avoidance of recently eaten foods by land hermit crabs, Coenobita compressus. Animal Behaviour, 55(2), 485-496.

Turra, A., & Denadai, M. R. (2004). Interference and exploitation components in interespecific competition between sympatric intertidal hermit crabs. Journal of Experimental Marine Biology and Ecology, 310(2), 183-193.

Vance, R. R. (1972). The role of shell adequacy in behavioral interactions involving hermit crabs. Ecology, 53(6), 1075-1083.

Vannini, M., & Ferretti, J. (1997).

Chemoreception in two species of terrestrial hermit crabs (Decapoda: Coenobitidae).Journal of Crustacean Biology, 17(1), 33-37.

Vermeij, G. J. (2012). Evolution: remodelling hermit shellters. Current biology, 22(20), R882-R884.

WADA, S., OHMORI, H., GOSHIMA, S., & NAKAO, S. (1997). Shell-size preference of hermit crabs depends on their growth rate. Animal Behaviour, 54(1), 1-8.

Williams, J. D., & McDermott, J. J. (2004). Hermit crab biocoenoses: a worldwide review of the diversity and natural history of hermit crab associates. Journal of experimental marine biology and ecology, 305(1), 1-128.

A	I	N	S	E	C	T	S	P	L	S	S	O
C	R	U	S	T	A	C	E	A	N	A	D	M
S	Q	W	C	Z	M	Q	D	A	O	L	F	N
D	M	E	A	X	O	W	E	S	C	T	G	I
F	O	R	V	C	U	E	C	D	T	W	H	V
G	L	T	E	V	F	R	A	F	U	A	J	O
H	T	Y	N	B	L	T	P	G	R	T	K	R
J	I	U	G	N	A	Y	O	H	N	E	L	O
K	N	I	E	M	G	U	D	J	A	R	O	U
L	G	O	R	V	E	I	O	K	L	A	P	S

CRUSTACEAN   SCAVENGER   OMNIVOROUS

CAMOUFLAGE   INSECTS   DECAPOD

NOCTURNAL   MOLTING   SALTWATER

Made in the USA
Las Vegas, NV
29 November 2023

81710829R00029